"Just One More"

When Desires Don't Take No for an Answer

Resources for Changing Lives

A Ministry of
THE CHRISTIAN COUNSELING AND
EDUCATIONAL FOUNDATION
Glenside, Pennsylvania

RCL Ministry Booklets
Susan Lutz, Series Editor

"Just One More"

When Desires Don't Take No for an Answer

Edward T. Welch

P&R
PUBLISHING
P.O. BOX 817 • PHILLIPSBURG • NEW JERSEY 08865-0817

Printed in the United States of America

Library of Congress Cataloging-in-Publication Data

Welch, Edward T., 1953-
    Just one more : when desires don't take no for an answer / Edward T. Welch.
        p. cm — (Resources for changing lives)
      ISBN 0-87552-689-6 (pbk.)
    1. Self-control—Religious aspects—Christianity.
2. Addicts—Religious life. I. Title. II. Series.

BV4647.S39 W45 2002
248.8'629—dc21

                                 2001059833

Want . . . want . . . want. It's the dripping faucet of the human soul. Sound familiar? It should. We want things. No, we *really* want them. We crave them. We want them so badly that we can physically *feel* our wants.

Pick one of your cravings for a moment. If you can't immediately think of one, stick with the usual suspects: something mind-altering, something sexual, or something related to food.

Chances are that you have said "no" at least once to these desires—"no" to a second dessert, "no" to the first drink, "no" to the late night visit to the local drug dealer, "no" to an opportunity for online pornography, or even "no" to thoughts and imaginations that have gotten out of hand. But sometimes our desires just don't take no for an answer.

No, I really shouldn't, we think.

Our good sense agrees. *I have been there before, and it wasn't pretty.*

Even our conscience chimes in: *Don't do it.*

But the deal is already done. It was probably decided long ago. We become overmatched by a desire that patiently urges, "Just this one time and then you can quit." Or it just plain demands, "GIVE ME WHAT I WANT AND GIVE IT TO ME NOW!" So we do just one more. It seems like the only way to satisfy the desire.

We aren't thinking about *ten* more. We aren't thinking that we want to devote our lives to that desire. Frankly, we aren't thinking much at all. We are thinking only about the moment, nothing more.

Will I get caught? Irrelevant question. The craving is what matters. Nothing else exists.

What does God say about this? With practice, you can avoid this one, but you'll have a tougher time with the lingering guilt.

Will this satisfy? No question here. *Yes, it will. It will definitely satisfy.*

So the cycle continues:

Imaginations → Cravings → Saying "yes."

I envision it, I desire it, I get it. The next step, of course, is "I am satisfied by it"—at least we think we *should* be. The cycle can't continue without some satisfaction, or at least the anticipation of it. But isn't it amazing how small a dose of satisfaction we are willing to settle for? In fact, "satisfaction" might not even be the right word. It is more that the craving has temporarily eased. We don't really experience that much long-lasting pleasure. But, as unsatisfying and hurtful as this cycle is, we figure that we can live with it. *Yes, it is a problem, but it is under control.*

Think again. Are you under *its* control?

This booklet is a brief opportunity to consider a cycle that has been called addictions. Like many other problems, we can see the cycle in other people, but it is tougher to see it in ourselves. When it gets personal, addictions run from careful inspection. They prefer to hide in the dark. When they can't hide any longer, they try to blend in as if they belong. They want to seem like a natural part of life. In fact, they want to appear so natural that they feel automatic, like waking up in the morning and mindlessly putting on the coffee. "Just do it," addictions preach. "Don't think."

But we must think, and we must think right. The stakes are high. It is as if we are at a crossroads. One road leads to life and blesses us; the other leads to death and curses us. This is no time to wander aimlessly.

When we stop and think, we realize that our desires—the seeds of addictions—are not always as innocent as they seem. To put it bluntly, they lie. Their agenda is to get what they want *now,* and they will go to any lengths to get it. What they hide is this basic law: the more we feed our desires, the bigger they become. At first, that doesn't make sense. If you feed something, it should be satisfied. But it is just the opposite. If we feed our desires, they become stronger. The pleasure is temporary. By the time we are done indulging ourselves, our desires are already saying, "That was nice; let's do it again." (Unless we feel guilty, in which case our desires might briefly hide until the guilt feelings have passed.)

The cycle either gets broken or it gets worse. One or the other.

So what do we do? Options seem limited. We tried to break the cycle before and it didn't last; why bother now? And, to be honest, "one more," even with all its misery, certainly beats "no more."

What a mess.

Yet change is possible. The links that hold this cycle together are ultimately spiritual links, and they can be broken. God himself assures it, and if God says it, then there is no question about it. The power to change is available. The problem is that even though we want to change . . . we don't want to change.

Do You *Want* to Change?

After surrendering to our cravings for awhile, *of course* we want to change. We feel guilty. Money is a problem. Relationships are worse. Misery is always knocking on the door. Lies are getting harder to remember, and it takes a genius to keep crafting more lies to cover up previous ones. Do you want to change? Yes.

But pause for a moment. Human beings want freedom. Change means putting up boundaries, and that doesn't feel very free. Add to this the fact that we crave something *because we like it.* Do you really think that a casual flirting with change will be enough? So think about it. Are you ready to change? Do you actually *want* to change? You are open to the idea of change, but what are your conditions?

- You want it, but without having to break a sweat.
- You want it because you are *supposed* to want it. Maybe you are not really thinking yet. You are moving around like a robot, just trying to please people.
- You want it, but not at the cost of saying goodbye to something you love.

- You want it—sometimes.
- You want it—tomorrow.
- You want it simply because it will make life a little easier or bring hope back to a relationship.
- You want it, but you are waiting for God to take away your cravings. Until he does, you feel as if there is nothing you can or should do, which is a convenient excuse for continuing.

If you recognize any of these mixed messages in your heart, you are blessed. God is with you. How can you know? When the light shines into areas of your life that usually prefer to stay in the dark, then you know that God is doing something. So let the light keep shining.

Start by being honest, not just with yourself but with someone else as well. Addictions thrive on privacy. They live in the shadows and don't want to be seen. They persuade you that you can do it on your own. But, here again, they lie. Don't listen to the dozens of reasons you could give for staying undercover. Think of some wise people—people who can speak the truth in love—and be open with them about your struggle. Get them to pray for you and teach you. Keep this rule of thumb: if you are resistant to telling someone else, then you *need* to tell someone else.

Your goal is to live publicly, out in the open. Imagine a life with no more lies, no more fears of being caught, no more feeling condemned. No more looking over your shoulder. Anyway, the reality is that our lives *are* public. Not only do other people often find us out, but God himself knows the hidden places of our hearts. We already are much more public than we think. If the Holy God sees us, it shouldn't make too much difference if other sinners like ourselves know something about our hearts.

Why Do You Want to Change?

So, let's assume that you are sitting on the fence. You want to change, but you don't want to change. Something has to get you off the fence. *Why* should you want to change? Since our motives and intentions are so important, we need a good reason. If you are trying to change because of pressure from family or friends, that isn't all bad, but it won't last. If you simply fear being caught, that *certainly* won't last. The only reason that can take us through the tough times is God.

It should be enough for God to simply say

to us, "Stop it." After all, God is God. He made us. He is not to be trifled with. But, for some reason, God speaks differently than we would expect. He is patient and speaks gently to us. He actually woos us like a bridegroom courting his bride. He tries to make a relationship with him look as attractive as it really is. He is the one who says "I love you" first. One way he does this is by inviting us to a banquet more wonderful than we could imagine.

> Come, all you who are thirsty,
>   come to the waters;
> and you who have no money,
>   come, buy and eat!
> Come, buy wine and milk
>   without money and without cost.
> Why spend money on what is not bread,
>   and your labor on what does not
>   satisfy?
> Listen, listen to me, and eat what is
>   good,
>   and your soul will delight in the
>   richest of fare. (Isaiah 55:1–2)

This is reason to change.

Have you ever received an invitation so beautiful? Probably not. When was the last time you were invited to something incredibly costly and the only thing you had to bring was *nothing*? If you did receive such an invitation, you would probably look for the fine print. There would have to be a catch. And there is.

The catch is that bringing nothing is too much for most people. We come to the door and offer sobriety, great sorrow, self-loathing, and promises to be better tomorrow. But God asks for nothing. In fact, he *requires* nothing. Anything else disrespects the greatness of God's generosity and underestimates the cost of the feast. It would be like slipping a buck to someone who just saved your life and telling him, "Here, have a cup of coffee on me."

If you want to do something, be humbled by the love bestowed on you. Be thankful for the gift you could never repay. Remember every day that it was not free. The reason we are able to enter with nothing is because Jesus Christ paid the full price for our entrance. This is why the cross of Christ is the focus of so much praise. It was there that Jesus paid our way to a banquet with the Father. We honor him when we simply believe and enter (John 6:29).

What happens when you hear someone talk about Jesus? The mention of his name should provoke something in you. If you weren't expecting it, what are you thinking? "Been there, done that"? "Jesus is fine, but what does that have to do with what I'm struggling with?" If you *were* expecting him to be brought up, does he nevertheless seem less and less relevant? Despite these reactions, the truth is that addictions are a spiritual problem. Yes, they are physical too, but they are spiritual at their very core. The struggles in our life always point back to our relationship with God. Whether it is hassles with a spouse, parents who didn't care, problems at work, or an addiction that rarely takes "no" for an answer, the way we live before others always points back to our relationship with God. If you are angry with other people, you are angry with God. If you believe you can get away with wrong thinking or behavior, it is because you don't believe that God is near. If you are careless with your life because you think there is no hope, then you don't believe that you are lovingly invited to the banquet.

If you aren't moved by the fact that God offers you this invitation, something is wrong that goes deeper than addictions. Your Creator loves you! Even though he knows you through and through, he desires to be with you. If you don't really care, then you are beginning to see how your life is an expression of your relationship with God. You prefer that God leave you alone. More than that, you are saying, "God, *I* want to be God." And you have already seen how hard that can be.

So are you stuck—on the fence? Some people *want* to be stuck because it gives them more time to indulge their addiction. Some people *want* to be hopeless because then their conscience can't condemn them for doing "one more." Some people *want* to be stuck because it beats worshipping God. Our motivations are trickier than we think. If we don't realize that they are mixed, we are lying to ourselves.

A change in behavior requires new motives. New motives take their first step by responding to God's invitation to the banquet. Not sure about this? Go public with your questions or your doubts. Bring what is hidden or quiet out into the open. Talk to someone whose walk with God you respect.

How Does Life Work?

If you acknowledge that your motives are mixed, that is a great step of honesty. If you add an openness to consider who Jesus Christ is, that is plenty. These are two basic steps that everyone needs to take. If you can say, "I can't trust myself, but I can trust Jesus," you are on the path of wisdom. But there is more. As you start to look more closely at Jesus Christ, you will see that he cares deeply about your personal struggles. He is not a king on a faraway throne. Instead, he calls himself Immanuel, which means God-with-us. He is God-with-us in the details of daily life. He is God-with-us who knows how life works, and he freely gives us wise, practical instruction. Here is a sampling of that wisdom as it relates to our struggles with addictions.

Get Help. You already know this, although that doesn't make it any easier to actually do it. But you can't go it alone.

- "The way of a fool seems right to him, but a wise man listens to advice." (Prov. 12:15)
- "Plans fail for lack of counsel, but with many advisors they succeed." (Prov. 15:22)
- "Listen to advice and accept instruction, and in the end you will be wise." (Prov. 19:20)

- "Two are better than one, because they have a good return for their work: If one falls down, his friend can help him up." (Eccl. 4:9–10)

Don't forget, addictions love to hide. They give dozens of reasons why they should stay private. Many of them sound persuasive, such as *I don't want to bother Bob; he's too busy already.* Don't listen to them. If you think about them, they are prideful: *I can do it on my own, thank you very much.* God's way of wisdom is that he uses people to help us.

Whom should you ask? Ask two people who know what the Bible says, listen well, speak the truth, and pray.

Don't be afraid to call things sin. For some reason, addicts don't like the word "sin." Of course, no one actually *likes* it, but people who talk about addictions really avoid it. They prefer "shortcomings." The word sin, however, reminds us that these shortcomings are actually disobedience against God. In Jeremiah 2:35, the Lord says, "I will pass judgment on you because you say, 'I have not sinned.'" First John 1:8 adds, "If we claim to be without sin, we deceive ourselves and the truth is not in us."

If we define sin as the violation of the Ten Commandments or the violation of the Golden Rule, then it's a fact that everyone sins every day. Without a doubt, some people are nicer than others, but no one consistently treats others—in word, thought, and deed—as we ourselves want to be treated. In fact, the best people are those who are more aware of their own faults. Good people are usually the ones who know they *aren't* good. They are quick to acknowledge their own faults or sins.

So to talk about sin is not unkind. It is just acknowledging the truth. In fact, to ignore wrongness in ourselves would be to practice self-deception, and this—especially when we talk about addiction—is exactly what we want to avoid. Does our wrongness offend our pride? Perhaps. But that is a small price to pay when self-deception and its destructive consequences are the alternative.

Now consider going one step further. According to the Bible, addictions is slavery, but it is also false pride, selfishness, unbelief, and lust (1 Cor. 5:11, 6:9–10; Gal. 5:19–21). In other words, the deepest problem in *addictions* is sin. There can certainly be physical problems as well, but give this some thought. Admittedly, the idea sounds old-fashioned at first. How can the experience of being out-of-control be sinful? You didn't want it. It wanted you. That certainly doesn't feel like sin.

But cravings and desires are not quite the same as an invading virus. If you catch a virus, you have no choice. You don't want it, and you would be glad to be rid of it. Addictions, however, don't just happen to us. We choose them. After a while, the addiction chooses us and we feel like slaves, but it is *voluntary* slavery.

As one older man observed, "When the desire for drink hits me, I feel like I am being pulled in different directions by two teams of horses."

"Which team wins?" asked a friend.

"Whichever one I say 'giddyap' tō."

Even with all the misery they bring, addictions do something for us. They might allow a brief opportunity to forget, punish ("drinking at" people), rage, cure self-consciousness and timidity, avoid pain, fill holes in one's self-image, adjust emotions, fit in with others, prove to yourself that you can do what you want, or keep loneliness at bay. Addictions don't just happen. They usually take time, effort, and practice.

Can you see what addictions have to do with God? The question that God puts to us is, *Whom will you worship? Me or idols?* Aren't the objects of our cravings modern idols? And like all idols, we hope they will give us what we want—power, pleasure, meaning, identity, revenge, escape. But idols don't play fair. They expect our full allegiance in return.

What can you do? Confess your sin to God. Even better, pray with a friend as you confess it to God.

Know that Jesus Christ forgives sin. If you are going to take sin seriously, you'd better take forgiveness just as seriously. Here is another rule of thumb: guilt makes real change impossible. If you aren't sure that Christ offers forgiveness—*complete* forgiveness—then you are guaranteed to remain stuck.

This might seem a long way from actually dealing with addictions, but it is a critical, foundational step. Skip this and you cannot succeed. God's Word teaches that if we keep falling back into our same old patterns, it is because we have forgotten that we have been cleansed from past sins (2 Peter 2:19).

Is it still hard to believe that you are forgiven as you turn to Christ?

- Perhaps you never really professed faith in Christ. You may know some facts about God but you never trusted fully in Christ's righteousness. You are still trying to pay God back.

- Perhaps you just can't believe that you could be so loved. If so, join the crowd! No one deserves God's love. That's what makes it amazing.

- Perhaps you are mad at yourself for repeating the same sin over and over. But isn't this a form of pride in which you think you can deal with sin on your own?

- Perhaps you are saying that you regret the consequences of your behavior. But just because consequences persist doesn't mean that you aren't forgiven.

- Perhaps you don't really believe that God the Father is satisfied by what Christ did on the cross. But God's Word is clear (Rom. 5:9; Eph. 1:7; 1 John 1:7; Rev. 1:5). Further evidence of God's satisfaction is Jesus' resurrection from the dead. His bodily resurrection was the Father's signal that the penalty for sin had been fully paid. Nothing remained to be done (Heb. 7:25). Just believe.

- Perhaps you simply do not *want* to believe you are forgiven. You may know there is forgiveness in Jesus, but you prefer guilt. Why? Because guilt has more of a pay-off than we think. For example, the religious sounding *I'm too bad to be forgiven* might be a veiled attempt to leave the door open for future drug use. It works this way: If you are not forgiven, then you can think that God has abandoned you, and if God has abandoned you, then you might as well continue with your addiction. Another deceptive possibility is: *My sins are so bad I should punish myself. What's the best way to punish myself? I will do it by continuing my addiction.*

- Perhaps you think you are just going to go back to your addiction eventually, so why bother being a hypocrite? In that case, forgiveness is not really the issue. You must go back to basics. Do you remember that addictions deceive us, so that we cannot trust our own thinking? Do you know that God is good? The cross proves it. Do you realize that (especially considering how often Scripture speaks of it) it is possible to get, and even enjoy, self-control? God actually wants to give it to us. Do you remember the tragedy that has been associated with sin? Or, as C. S. Lewis asks, do you prefer playing in mud puddles when God offers you a holiday at the beach? You need to be persuaded that God is more desirable than anything on earth (Ps. 73:25).

Here is a way to see if you know God's forgiveness: Do you have ongoing, heartfelt thanks in your heart to God? This is how you respond when you receive a wonderful gift. If this doesn't feel familiar, get help. Get wise people to pray for you and teach you about what Jesus did for you.

Develop a plan. The path of wisdom is a thoughtful one. Those who walk in it don't aimlessly wander; they consider their ways (Prov. 6:6), listen to counsel (Prov. 15:22), and act on what they know is true (James 1:22). With the foundation of what God has done clearly in your mind, it is time to come up with a plan that includes figuring out how to work, love, rest, resolve conflicts, and master the other ordinary details of daily living. One of the details is dealing with cravings and addictions.

If you don't have a plan, it might be because you don't *know* a plan. But what is more likely is that you want to let your addiction find its way back into your life. It is as if you crossed the bridge from slavery into the Promised Land, but you didn't burn the bridge behind you. So *act* on your desire to change. Put up a fight. Burn the bridge. Develop a plan.

Keep it simple at first.

- I will sever all contact with drug buddies.
- Once a week I will have someone check the internet sites I hit.
- I will make my eating public by eating with family or a friend every night.

The idea is to examine the steps you take to get to your addiction. Addictive behavior doesn't just happen. It starts an hour, a day, or a week before. You don't just get mysteriously transported to a place where you are likely to satisfy your addictive desires. You have a map.

For example, you might begin by reflecting on how bad your life is. Then you start feeling depressed; then you feel hopeless; then you remember how your addictive behavior was satisfying in the past; then you imagine what it would be like to do it again. At some point in this process, it is too late to turn back. You need a plan that will barricade you from getting to Step Two. Don't wait until you get to Step Ten.

Make this plan concrete. Don't say, "I'm going to call Janet and ask if she would pray for me." Say, "I will call Janet by Tuesday night. I will tell her what I am struggling with, and I will ask her if she will pray for me for the next month." If your plan isn't specific, you will be giving yourself room to wiggle out of it.

Be sure to include a strategy for knowing more about the triune God—Father, Son, and Holy Spirit. The reality is that you know God much less than you think. For example, you think he is trying to *keep* you from pleasure rather than *give* you pleasure. (Take a look at all the times the word *delight* shows up in the Bible). You think he doesn't see every aspect of your life at all times (but everything is laid bare before him). You think he loves you less than he does (yet he gave his only Son in order to have a relationship with you). You think sin is not that big a deal to him (but it is so heinous that the penalty was death). You think that he does not have the power to change you (even though he has the power to raise the dead).

If addictions, at their root, are all about who or what we are going to worship, then Jesus Christ has got to become much more attractive to you than any other false god, such as drugs, sex, or food. The reality, of course, is that Jesus *is* more attractive. It is a matter of seeing everything more clearly. How does this happen? With the willingness to be suspicious of your old assumptions, with the help of others, with asking God to show us more of himself, with searching the Scriptures and not stopping until we have found Jesus Christ to be more beautiful than we once thought.

One word of caution: If you are expecting an immediate, mountaintop experience, be careful. God certainly gives these, but *his* plan is that they come as we persist in seeking him. His plan values our faithful efforts. So don't give up. It is worth the effort. As Augustine said, "You have made us for yourself, and our heart is restless until it finds its rest in you" (Confessions 1.1).

Remember, the battle is good. A thirty-eight-year-old husband and father was ready to quit. He felt as if he had been battling his desire for alcohol his entire adult life, and he was tired. *Where is the power of God?* he thought. *What about this victorious life that Christians talk about?* He didn't understand that the battle is good.

When it feels like a battle, that is a sign that something is right.

"The violent take it by force" is how the King James Version puts it (Matt. 11:12). That is the way God works. Every disciple of Christ is in a battle, one that demands spiritual strength and ongoing vigilance. This is where the language of disease is weak. It doesn't lend itself to violence—vigilance maybe, but not violence. When you are doing battle with sin, it requires preparation and a desire to absolutely eradicate it. This is not peacetime! The goal is to develop a battle-like, aggressive, rigorous, take-no-prisoners style of life.

Like all battles, this will take time. In fact, get ready to fight for the rest of your life. That's the way it is for every believer. But don't let the length of the battle scare you. All you have to do is *fight the battle today*. God will give you all the strength you need.

What makes it easier is that you are on the winning side. Your situation is a lot like ancient Israel's: God delivered them from Egypt, but then they had to fight to take the Promised Land.

> I [the Lord] have come down to rescue
> them from the hand of the Egyptians

and to bring them up out of that land
into a good and spacious land, a land
flowing with milk and honey. (Ex.3:8)

This was God's promise. He said that he
would bring his people out of slavery and give
them a land that was their own. *The land was
theirs.* Those who trust in Christ have gone
through an even more dramatic deliverance.
Through the wonder of Spirit-wrought faith,
we are united to Christ. What was his is now
ours, and the sin that was ours has been
placed on him. We died with Christ to the
penalty and power of sin, and now we are
raised with Christ to live for God as his
beloved children.

Scripture then makes very bold statements
about our life in Christ. It almost seems to sug-
gest that we don't sin anymore. Romans 6:6
says that "our old self was crucified with him so
that the body of sin might be done away with,
that we should no longer be slaves to sin."
This, however, is similar to God saying that
the land belonged to Israel. They were promised the land, but *they still had to fight for it.* Fur-
thermore, not all the battles were successful.
There were times when Israel fought without
the Lord himself leading them into battle, and

they lost. There are times when we, too, might take our eyes off Jesus and lose a battle, but, like Israel, we have been promised something truly remarkable. We are promised a new life, and then we are told to fight for it. And the fight is worth it.

This is a lot to think about—maybe too much for one sitting. Yet, as you might anticipate, there is even more good news that could be shared. God is very generous in teaching us how to walk a wise path through life. What you have just read is only a sketchy map that highlights the important landmarks. But God's wisdom is available to us all. If things get overwhelming and complex, and you are getting lost in the details, think about the thing that is most important: God sacrificed his own Son for us. We have been freed from the domination of our cruel taskmasters and instead, we now belong to him.

- "You are not your own; you were bought with a price." (1 Cor. 6:19–20)
- "And he [Jesus Christ] died for all, that those who live should no longer live for themselves but for him who died for them and was raised again." (2 Cor. 5:15)

This is called the Gospel. It is the best news we could ever hear. It's more than enough to win the battle against "just one more."

Edward T. Welch *directs the School of Biblical Counseling at the Christian Counseling and Educational Foundation in Glenside, Pennsylvania, where he is a counselor and faculty member.*

RCL Ministry Booklets

A.D.D.: Wandering Minds and Wired Bodies, by Edward T. Welch

Anger: Escaping the Maze, by David Powlison

Angry at God? Bring Him Your Doubts and Questions, by Robert D. Jones

Depression: The Way Up When You Are Down, by Edward T. Welch

Domestic Abuse: How to Help, by David Powlison, Paul David Tripp, and Edward T. Welch

Forgiveness: "I Just Can't Forgive Myself!" by Robert D. Jones

God's Love: Better than Unconditional, by David Powlison

Guidance: Have I Missed God's Best? by James C. Petty

Homosexuality: Speaking the Truth in Love, by Edward T. Welch

"Just One More": When Desires Don't Take No for an Answer, by Edward T. Welch

Marriage: Whose Dream? by Paul David Tripp

Motives: "Why Do I Do the Things I Do?" by Edward T. Welch

Pornography: Slaying the Dragon, by David Powlison

Pre-Engagement: 5 Questions to Ask Yourselves, by David Powlison and John Yenchko